W9-BWU-562

Date: 1/23/12

J 552 ALL
Allen, Nancy Kelly,
Minerals and rocks /

PALM BEACH COUNTY
LIBRARY SYSTEM
3650 SUMMIT BLVD.
WEST PALM BEACH, FL 33406

Rock It!™

MINERALS AND ROCKS

Nancy Kelly Allen

PowerKiDS press™

New York

For Cory

Published in 2009 by The Rosen Publishing Group, Inc.
29 East 21st Street, New York, NY 10010

Copyright © 2009 by The Rosen Publishing Group, Inc.

All rights reserved. No part of this book may be reproduced in any form without permission in writing from the publisher, except by a reviewer.

First Edition

Editor: Amelie von Zumbusch
Book Design: Kate Laczynski
Photo Researcher: Jessica Gerweck

Photo Credits: Cover, pp. 1, 4, 6, 8, 12, 14, 16 Shutterstock.com; p. 10 © Altrendo Nature/Getty Images; p. 18 © Dea Picture Library/Getty Images; p. 20 © Getty Images.

Library of Congress Cataloging-in-Publication Data

Allen, Nancy Kelly, 1949–
  Minerals and rocks / Nancy Kelly Allen. — 1st ed.
     p. cm. — (Rock it!)
  Includes index.
  ISBN 978-1-4358-2761-5 (library binding) — ISBN 978-1-4358-3184-1 (pbk.)
ISBN 978-1-4358-3190-2 (6-pack)
  1. Minerals—Juvenile literature. 2. Rocks—Juvenile literature. I. Title.
  QE365.2.A66 2009
  552—dc22
                                    2008034466

Manufactured in the United States of America

CONTENTS

Some of the salt people eat comes from mines. Salt is also made from seawater. People have used salt for over 5,000 years.

Who Needs Minerals?

Minerals, who needs them? You do. Everyone needs minerals every day. The salt in your food is a mineral, called halite. Many types of toothpaste have a mineral called fluorite in them.

Minerals are solid matter that occur naturally but are not alive. Minerals are most often found in rocks. In fact, rocks are made of minerals. Some rocks are made of only one kind of mineral. For example, pure pieces of the rock marble are made of a mineral called calcite. However, most rocks are made of two or more minerals. More than 3,000 different minerals can be found in Earth's rocks.

The mineral pyrite is made from the elements iron and sulfur. Pyrite is also known as fool's gold because it looks like the more expensive mineral gold.

Beautiful Crystals

Did you know that gold is a mineral? A few minerals, such as gold, silver, and iron, are made of just one element. Elements are matter that cannot be broken down into other kinds of matter. Most minerals are compounds, or matter that is made of two or more elements combined. For example, the mineral hematite is made from the elements iron and oxygen.

The elements in minerals form crystals. Crystals are solids that grow in a set shape, such as a cube. The crystals in each kind of mineral always form in the same shape.

Take a close look at a tiny grain of salt. Each grain is shaped like a cube. This is because each grain of salt is a crystal.

Sometimes magma escapes to Earth's surface, where it is known as lava. Like magma, lava forms igneous rocks when it hardens.

Changing Rocks

Many of Earth's rocks are made of minerals that were around when dinosaurs lived! This is because rocks take a very long time to form. Earth has three kinds of rocks. They are called igneous rocks, sedimentary rocks, and metamorphic rocks. These rocks slowly change as they move through Earth's rock cycle.

Inside Earth, heat and **pressure** change the minerals in igneous and sedimentary rocks. This forms metamorphic rocks. When the heat and pressure under ground become even greater, rocks melt into **magma**. Igneous rocks form when magma hardens. Sedimentary rocks form from sediment, or matter that builds up over time. This sediment is usually bits of older rock.

The reddish spots in this rock are garnets.
Garnets come in many colors. They form
in both metamorphic and igneous rocks.

How Do Minerals Form?

Many rocks **contain** pockets of a single mineral. These pockets often form along with the rocks around them. Some minerals, such as rubies, form as magma cools into igneous rock. Rubies are red stones used to make **jewelry**. The heat and pressure that form metamorphic rocks can turn existing minerals into new minerals. Rocks known as jade form this way. Jade is often made into jewelry.

Other minerals form in hot springs, where hot water that is full of **dissolved** minerals flows to Earth's **surface** from under ground. In time, the water dries up, leaving minerals behind.

You can grow sugar crystals. Just stir 2 cups (450 g) of sugar into 1 cup (.2 l) of hot water. Then, drop a string into the water. As the water dries up, crystals will form on the string.

New Mexico's Carlsbad Caverns National Park has dozens of caves and is full of beautiful mineral formations.

Every Little Drop

Can dripping water form rocks? Yes, it can, drip by drip. When water drips through holes in certain caves, it can produce beautiful mineral formations. Many of these formations are created by calcite in limestone caves. Limestone is a sedimentary rock made of calcite. When rainwater drips through soil and then limestone, some of the limestone's calcite dissolves in the water. Calcite crystals form and are **deposited** on the cave's walls, roof, and floor.

Cave formations come in many shapes and colors. Most are calcite deposits, but they can also be made of the minerals aragonite and gypsum.

Stalactites are mineral formations that point down from a cave's roof, while stalagmites point up from the floor. Draperies are thin, wavy sheets of calcite.

The quartz sand found on most beaches and in many deserts is also known as silica. People use silica to make many things, such as glass.

Clear as Crystal

Have you ever walked on a sandy beach? Sand forms from rocks that break down over time. Most sand is made of quartz, the most common mineral on Earth's surface. Quartz can be found in sedimentary rocks, igneous rocks, and metamorphic rocks.

Other minerals are commonly found in just one kind of rock. For example, the dark green mineral olivine is generally found in igneous rocks, such as basalt. Metamorphic rocks often contain special minerals, called index minerals. Index minerals help scientists figure out how much heat and pressure the rocks were under when they formed.

Quartz comes in many colors. Clear quartz is called rock crystal. Long ago, crystal balls were made from clear quartz. Purple quartz, known as amethyst, makes beautiful jewelry.

Purple quartz is known as amethyst.
As all kinds of quartz do, amethysts
have hexagonal, or six-sided, crystals.

Clues

Minerals often look alike. However, geologists, or people who study rocks, use the **properties** of minerals to figure out which minerals are which. One property they study is luster, or how minerals shine. For example, the minerals topaz and emerald shine like glass, while graphite has a dull luster.

Crystal habit, or the special shape each mineral's crystals take, is another clue geologists use to recognize minerals. Silver crystals are always in a cube shape. Geologists also study a mineral's cleavage, or how it breaks. The mineral muscovite splits in one direction into flat **layers**. Fluorite splits into pieces shaped like diamonds. Quartz breaks into pieces with round edges.

The mineral hemimorphite comes in many colors, such as green, white, brown, yellow, and blue. However, it always leaves a white streak when rubbed on a white tile.

More Clues

Color is another clue that geologists use to recognize minerals. Sulfur is a mineral that is always yellow. Other minerals, such as fluorite, come in many colors. However, some minerals appear one color in daylight and glow a different color in **ultraviolet** light. This is called **fluorescence**. Fluorite always glows blue in ultraviolet light. A mineral's streak, or the color it leaves behind when rubbed against a white tile, is another clue. Fluorite always leaves a white streak.

Geologists also test how hard minerals are. They use a tool called Mohs' scale to measure a mineral's hardness. Talc is the softest mineral. All other minerals can **scratch** talc.

The size of diamonds is measured in carats.
This man is holding up the world's largest uncut
diamond. The diamond weighs 616 carats.

Diamonds Are Forever

Diamonds are the world's hardest minerals. These stones can scratch all other minerals, but no other minerals can scratch diamonds. Because diamonds are so hard, bits of diamond are on the tips of dentists' drills.

Diamonds are often used to make jewelry. Many diamonds are cut at different angles to show a rainbow of colors as light hits them. Most of these expensive stones are clear.

Billions of years ago, diamonds formed deep under ground under very high heat and pressure. These stones are sometimes brought to Earth's surface by **volcanoes**. Diamonds are so hard that even hot magma cannot melt them.

A Use for Everything

Minerals are all around us. Many useful metals, such as iron, silver, and copper, are minerals. When you turn on the lights, copper wires carry electricity. People also mix minerals to make cement. Cement holds together bricks in buildings. The mineral mica is found in most rocks. It is used to make computers. Quartz is used to make glue, glass, and paint. Paint also often contains talc.

People also have minerals in their bodies. We all need minerals to live. We get most of the minerals we need from food. Milk has calcium, and fruit has potassium. Minerals are an important part of our daily lives.

GLOSSARY

billions (BIL-yunz) Thousands of millions. One billion is 1,000 millions.

contain (kun-TAYN) To hold or to have.

deposited (dih-PAH-zut-ed) Left behind.

dissolved (dih-ZOLVD) Mixed totally into a liquid.

fluorescence (flu-REH-sents) Glowing when hit by waves of light that people cannot see.

jewelry (JOO-ul-ree) Objects worn on the body that are made of special metals, such as gold and silver, and valued stones.

layers (LAY-erz) Thicknesses of something.

magma (MAG-muh) Hot, melted rock inside Earth.

pressure (PREH-shur) A force that pushes on something.

properties (PRAH-pur-teez) Things that describe something.

scratch (SKRACH) To rub or tear the surface of something.

surface (SER-fes) The outside of anything.

ultraviolet (ul-truh-VY-uh-let) Having to do with light people cannot see.

volcanoes (vol-KAY-nohz) Openings that sometimes shoot up hot, melted rock called lava.

INDEX

WEB SITES

Due to the changing nature of Internet links, PowerKids Press has developed an online list of Web sites related to the subject of this book. This site is updated regularly. Please use this link to access the list:
www.powerkidslinks.com/rockit/minerals/